The organisation of media

The organisation of media

BERNARD CHIBNALL

CLIVE BINGLEY
LONDON

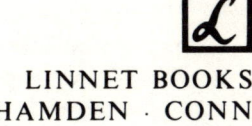
LINNET BOOKS
HAMDEN · CONN

FIRST PUBLISHED 1976 IN THE UK BY CLIVE BINGLEY LTD
16 PEMBRIDGE ROAD LONDON W11
SIMULTANEOUSLY PUBLISHED IN THE USA BY LINNET BOOKS
AN IMPRINT OF THE SHOE STRING PRESS INC
995 SHERMAN AVENUE HAMDEN CONNECTICUT 06514
SET IN 12 ON 14 BEMBO AND
PHOTOSET, PRINTED AND BOUND IN THE UK BY
REDWOOD BURN LTD TROWBRIDGE AND ESHER
COPYRIGHT © BERNARD CHIBNALL 1976
ALL RIGHTS RESERVED
CLIVE BINGLEY ISBN: 0–85157–212–X
LINNET BOOKS ISBN: 0–208–01525–6

Library of Congress Cataloging in Publication Data

Chibnall, Bernard.
    The organisation of media.

    Includes bibliographical references and index.
    1. Libraries—Special collections—Non-book materials.
    2. Instructional materials centers.
I. Title.
Z688.N6C45   1976   025.17'7   75-37930
ISBN 0–208–01525–6 (Linnet)

Contents

	page
Preface	7
Chapter	
I Education and communication	9
II Function in theory	14
III Function in practice	22
IV Organisation	30
V Staff	38
VI Facilities	48
VII Storage and access	55
VIII Conclusion	65
References	76
Index	79

Preface

This book reflects my personal experience and it should be set into perspective. I learned my craft as a librarian in the Kodak Research Library and transferred after three years to the Production Library of the Shell Film Unit. I was always impressed by the smoothness of the change and the ease with which the rules of book librarianship and information work could be applied to the world of film. It consequently concerned me greatly when, many years later, I found librarians and teachers wishing to treat non-book materials as something quite different from books.

As Director of the Media Unit in the University of Sussex I have had the pleasure of receiving many visitors and during the course of these meetings I have discussed many aspects of the organisation of media. It has been possible to identify some common themes and as these have evolved they appear to have been of interest to the librarians, producers and teachers I have met. It seemed therefore that I should attempt to set them down in writing.

The purpose of the book is not to set out detailed instructions for the organisation of media. These exist in other books already. My purpose here is to try to develop the underlying principles behind the processes of organisation, so that we may be better able to see the common purpose which the librarian, resource manager, producer or, for that matter, teacher should be trying to serve.

I am indebted to many colleagues and friends with whom I have collaborated over the years, who in their activities and discussions have helped me to develop my ideas. In particular, I must mention the late Sir Arthur Elton, who invited me into film librarianship in 1949. His acute sense of the problems of communication, his authoritative skill as a film director and his practical experience of organising his unique collection of illustrative material on railway history made him an ideal guide, philosopher and friend.

Most of all I must thank my family who have contributed so much to my enlightenment. Without their information, comment and pertinent questions my own thinking would have been that much less clear. My daughter Jennifer, in particular, has not only provided useful references but has cast a sharp eye over the early chapters. The imperfections which remain are of course my responsibility.

Finally, it is a pleasure to thank Gillian de Jong for patiently typing the text for me.

BERNARD CHIBNALL

Hove
Sussex

CHAPTER I

Education and communication

In the last few years the choice of material available to the teacher has increased both in variety and quantity. No longer are we restricted so closely to the printed word. The discourse of teaching, although still predominantly literary, can now be extended to embrace visual and aural media. In addition, equipment has been produced, at a price which educational institutions can afford, which uses such material and, perhaps even more important, produces it. As a result there has been a great deal of discussion, sometimes quite acrimonious, about how this material and equipment should be handled and organised. There has been a suggestion that the availability of audiovisual material as a resource created an entirely new situation in education (despite the work of Comenius[1] published in 1658), and that, as a consequence, teachers at all levels should develop new concepts of what education is all about.

It is an unfortunate aspect of the development of new ideas in education that it often seems necessary to their proponents that they be treated as totally innovatory, which is not only arrogant but inaccurate. If they are to be effective, new developments must be consciously based upon the various conditions of existing practices to which they are applied. (Even if a development goes so far as to be a total rejection, this in itself represents a relationship, albeit possibly unconscious, with existing practice.) Further, developments are more likely to find acceptance if they can in some way be related to existing practices than will be the case if they are presented as totally new ideas.

The view expressed here is that the availability of audiovisual materials represents an extension of the resources available for learning, and that their use represents a natural development of all that has been imaginative and inspiring in education over the years. The arguments about their organisation arise partly because characteristics of difference are being exaggerated at the expense of similarities, and partly because not all teachers use the resources available to them as much as they should. Even the standard orthodox book collection in school or public library is often under-utilised, and far too few teachers seem willing or able to incorporate audiovisual materials into their work. In the pages that follow an attempt is made to outline a philosophy which unites the conceptions involved in using resources and libraries, in producing materials and in the process of education, and to suggest how it can be applied to the organisation of media.

Let us start with a consideration of education and communication. It is commonplace these days to attribute many of the faults and failings of society to a breakdown of communication. So much so that the serious study of communication is inhibited by the fact that it appears to some that successful communication is the contemporary panacea. But effective communication is not a definable and repeatable product whose qualities are permanently established and universally applicable. It is a process which will change as we study it, whose significance and relevance will fluctuate, and to whose variations we must ourselves adapt in our own reactions and responses. The transfer of information may be measurable, the communicator may well feel content that his message has been received, and indeed this may be the case. The recipient may be able, when asked, to repeat back precisely what he has been told. But we deceive ourselves as communicators if we think that that is all that is involved. We have no easy means of determining how the recipient has 'seen' the information, or the context in which he has interpreted it. The process of interpreting and applying the information is irrevocably in his hands.

Communication is a game we play. Some of the rules are accepted by both sides; some are known only to one side, and if known to the other would not be accepted. We attach to words meanings which may or may not be understood by our readers or listeners. If they are understood they may not be agreed. In committees the chairman applies the rules and seeks their clarification. In a dialogue there is no chairman and the participants must themselves ensure that they understand each other's rules and meanings. Understanding is a change in appreciation which facilitates further understanding, and so the process of communication goes on.

We sometimes seem to think of communication as bridging a gap—a process whose end is determined. Rather should it take possession of a space in which interactions occur, and these interactions in turn define the area within which the communication process can develop.

The process of education is a process of communication. To become educated is to evolve a relationship with all that has been achieved in man's history, and to direct ourselves towards the possibilities of the future. We are subjected to the influence of writers through their books, poems and plays; of teachers who guide us individually in our studies; of designers, producers and other creative artists who involve us in aural and visual media. In the process of communication there is a positive relationship in which we respond to their stimuli and take possession of these influences. We do so by integrating them with the knowledge and understanding we already have. We in fact communicate with ourselves.

In so doing we extend our knowledge and understanding by a process of association. We link the new with the old and perhaps thereby change our concept of the old. This is an intensely personal process, since its progress will depend entirely on our individual understanding, our personal experience, our personality, our interests and the knowledge we already have.

We can thus distinguish two aspects of the communication process: the external and the internal, and an awareness of the distinction helps our understanding of the educational process.

Unless the teacher, producer or librarian is aware of the fact that the learner will process what he is offered, into a new structure within the context of his own system of associations, there is almost certain to be no real communication between them. It is easy to assume that successful communication has been achieved when a precise reflection is obtained from the person with whom we are in communication. Rather should we seek to cause a process of diffraction whose multiple images indicate that our expression has been processed by the receiver.

On the other hand, if the educational process is allowed to proceed without any specific checks on instruction (*ie*, precise reflections) only woolliness will result. The danger is that too great a concentration on measured results, and hence on defined ends, leads to a restriction of the educational process. We concentrate on filling gaps in the learner's information, rather than on creating spaces in which he can develop his knowledge. The process of diffracting information into new knowledge will be inhibited.

This argument implies a distinction between instruction and education. The former is to transmit information which must be accurately reflected by the learner; the latter involves the responsive process which develops in the individual. From this point of view it makes more sense to refer to instructional technology than to educational technology. The use of technology implies a method of attaining a given objective (*ie*, the attempt to fill a gap in someone's knowledge). The results can therefore be tested. If we treat education as a process as distinct from a method (*ie*, the creation of spaces into which the mind can expand rather than the closing of gaps), it cannot be predetermined, and it is therefore impossible to treat it in technological terms.

The problem in all communication is to sustain the balance between the processes of instruction and those of education. On many occasions this may well present itself as a dilemma, but it should always be regarded as a creative process. We are not in fact caught on the horns of a dilemma but, like the spider, use them as supports for the web we weave between them. It is the purpose of this book to suggest that the awareness of this process of sustaining the balance must underlie our organising of media, and that the process of organising can itself help us to achieve a greater awareness.

The importance of this cannot be overemphasised, for the balance is at the heart of the whole educational process. It is vital in the formal learning process between teacher and pupil, but also in all situations where we are faced, as we are continually, with the need to make a decision and with the problem of determining how much information is necessary for that decision to be effective.

CHAPTER II

Function in theory

When we set out to organise media we are concerned to make available information and structures. We do so having in mind that someone will take up this new information and add it to his own, and hence develop his knowledge. Let us consider this process in more detail.

If we intend to add something to someone's knowledge, it is useful if we first consider what form our knowledge takes. There is a tendency to think of knowledge as consisting of discrete facts or items, perhaps like pebbles in a bucket to which can be added further facts or pebbles which thus gradually build up the sum of our knowledge. This is certainly not the case. Each new item of information, if it is retained, links in with something already in our mind. It is both associated with something already there and brings with it a set of new associations. We learn through association: meaning is derived from relationships. When we are presented with new information we associate it with something we already know. We must do this, for otherwise the new item has no meaning. The meaning of the new item cannot stand in isolation. As I A Richards says[2] '(meanings) do so mind their company.' Roland Barthes has also made this point. In an interview with Stephen Heath[3] he says 'Only today I was reading a magnificent text by Brecht on Chinese painting in which he says that Chinese painting places things side by side, the one by the side of the other. It is a very simple formula, but also a very beautiful one, and very true, and what I am looking for, at bottom, is exactly this feeling of the "by the side of".'

Saussure[4] proffered a similar point in linguistics. In considering words, he distinguished between the word's signification and its value. The value can only be determined within the context in which the word is used. A piece of information has a signifying capacity in itself, but it only has value when it is seen in a context. In considering communication we must be aware of the fact that the same information will be being used in a different context by the persons in communication. If we see a bunch of flowers it signifies a bunch of flowers, but we have no idea of its value unless we also know whether it is intended for a bride, a coffin or as a gesture to an artist at the end of a concert. To value the bunch of flowers we must know the context. To give value to a statement we need to know its context.

In the process of education the learner will not necessarily associate the item with the same context as the teacher; nor will the user identify with the context of the librarian. Herein lies the major pitfall in any teaching/learning situation. Surely all of us have experienced a casual remark which has reminded us of a series of incidents far removed from the mind of the person making the remark—and perhaps if it was in school we have been rebuked for lack of attention! We have each of us our own structure of knowledge into which we fit the new as we acquire it. Even if we are given instruction, when we may be more closely linked to the work of the instructor, we shall still be fitting what we are taught into our own natural structure.

But it is not only the learner who has a structure in his mind. The teacher too has his own, which will stylise his presentation and determine the way in which he presents the content of his argument. Finally, and in our present context most importantly, the medium in which the information is presented also has a form or 'structure' which will affect the associations we make with the information which is presented. The context within which information is set will differ depending upon whether the information is written, spoken, illustrated with diagrams, charts, pictures and so on.

An obvious example of this is the difficulty one finds in turning a spoken statement into a written one. No new information is added, the final conclusions will be the same, but the effort needed to translate the statement from one form into the other is considerable. It follows that a significant process is taking place in the brain and that the different form of presentation represents a significant additional mental effort. It seems reasonable therefore to deduce that the way in which we receive new information affects the context in which we see it. The organisation inherent in a medium of presentation affects our appreciation of it.

This principle applies at all levels of organisation. A book will give us a different context from a film; an article in a journal will give us a different context from a lecture. Further, the way in which a collection of material is organised, for example, in a library will also affect our view of the subject. We frequently express this by our comments on classification schemes.

It is suggested in this analysis therefore that we should think of a learning situation as containing different structures of knowledge, *ie*, different associative patterns applying to the teacher, the student and to the means by which they are brought into contact with each other—the communication system or medium. The learning process itself is that in which these different structures interplay one with the other until new associations have been set up in the mind of the learner and, of course, of the teacher. If he has personal contact with the student, it is evident that the student's reaction will affect the teacher, but even if he is writing a textbook, or making a film, or any other form of presentation, his attitude to his subject is likely to change as the work proceeds. This is a common experience of subject specialists who work on films or television productions.

There may be a tendency to think that the variety of associations introduced by using different forms of presentation is a weakness, but this is far from being the case. It is the variety which is their strength and the reason for teachers at all levels of education turning to different kinds of presentation. I A Richards[5] quotes from Dr Johnson: 'It is not sufficiently considered that men more frequently require to be reminded than informed'. A different style of presentation can do just that. No new information need necessarily be offered, but by presenting it in a different form we remind people of what they know but perhaps do not understand in that context. The reminder will help their understanding. This process is crucial to teaching, where we must seek to build on what the student already knows and encourage him to think about it.

This approach is, of course, very demanding of the teacher, and anyone may be forgiven if in a large class he feels unable to adopt this approach wholeheartedly. He must be prepared to take up an entirely new set of associations unforeseen by him in his preparatory work, yet seized upon by his class or by some of them. This is particularly difficult if the class is working to an examination timetable, when such new ideas may well have no examinable significance. The freedom given to UK primary schools by the abolition of the 11-plus examination clearly demonstrates the advantages of allowing children to develop their own ideas. However it also demonstrates the disadvantages, for freedom cannot function without some rules, and certainly some primary schools and primary school teachers leave too many decisions to be made by the child, with the result that he floats in a fog of uncertainty.

At the other extreme, universities often seek to give their students great freedom in their studies when they should be in a position to use it. Nevertheless, even here some rules are necessary, and undoubtedly contemporary student unrest is partly generated by the uncertainties of the organisational system in which students and staff find themselves. However, since by this level this reflects the uncertainties of society as a whole, we should perhaps not be too hard on a community which in studying, reflects society and finds itself unable to lay down hard and fast rules. The problem of striking a balance between rules and freedom, or instruction and education, has already been referred to and underlies the whole of this book.

The relationship between information and instruction on the one hand, and understanding and education on the other, is paralleled in linguistics by Saussure's distinction between two forms of mental activity—the syntagmatic and the associative. The syntagmatic relations arise when we are linking elements in a linear way. In language we cannot pronounce two elements simultaneously: one follows the other, a close parallel to the way in which we convey information. On the other hand we have associative relationships where an element will call into mind simultaneously a host of other elements. As Saussure[6] says 'these are not supported by linearity. Their seat is in the brain; they are part of the inner storehouse that makes up the language of each speaker.' In our discussion, we are suggesting that facts are part of the inner storehouse that make up the understanding of each person. They are part of our own private contexts.

Ornstein,[7] an American psychologist, has considered the experimental evidence for these two activities to be associated with different halves of the brain. It appears that it is possible to link analytic thinking, *eg* language and logic, using ordered sequences, with the left hand side of the brain, whilst the right hand side can be linked with the ability to orientate in space, with artistic talents, awareness and recognition. It integrates material simultaneously rather than consecutively, in a line. It is not suggested that the two halves of the brain are exclusively concerned with these characteristics, but rather that they may be treated as specialising in these activities. Ornstein suggests that our culture in the West gives an emphasis to the verbal, intellectual abilities, and 'this bias intrudes into the most "objective" haunts of science'. We tend to undervalue the craftsman, the artist or the musician, who is apparently using the right side of his brain. He goes on to suggest 'that a complete human consciousness should include both modes of thought'.

Surely this integration is nowhere more necessary than in any process of communication, be it teaching or librarianship, when we must use all the artistry of which we are capable to convey the logic of a subject.

A powerful example of the combination of factual observation with the artistic skill of the poet is quoted by F H Ludlam,[8] Professor of Metereology at Imperial College, London. He discusses the description of the 'sudden onset of the Mediterranean winter' given in Shelley's 'Ode to the West Wind', and points out many 'poetic' descriptions which indicate how precisely Shelley had observed the phenomena. He states that: 'As a concise statement of the form and nature of the travelling thunderstorm, one of Nature's most complicated and still imperfectly understood phenomena, Shelley's description is unrivalled in English literature, even, until very recently, in scientific accounts'. As Sidney[9] says, 'A perfect picture I say, for he yieldeth to the powers of the mind an image of that whereof the philosopher bestoweth but a wordish description, which doth neither strike, pierce, nor possess the sight of the soul so much as that other doth'.

Clearly, few of us will lay claim to the perception and poetic imagination of a Shelley. Yet if we can find other ways of expressing ourselves, it may be that we can at least enhance our perception and elucidate our ideas with different images. It is a thesis of this text that the most important benefit to be derived from audiovisual materials is that they provide in their use and in their production just such another way of expressing ourselves. We have already referred to the common experience gained from working in films or television, that it gives a new insight into the subject matter; but it will also be clear to anyone who has handled a substantial enquiry for information or help in a library, that a similar creative discussion will often take place between the librarians and the subject expert. The material available, from its own internal structure, 'interferes' with the enquirer's own structure for the material in such a way as to raise questions which may well not previously have arisen. One can of course regard the phenomenon as 'interference' in a pejorative sense: stopping the process which one wants to follow. However those of us who have worked in different media would generally agree that, more often than not, the 'interference' should be regarded as a filter whose variable selectivity enhances our appreciation of the subject.

The enquirer may well be able to prepare materials or consult the library or resource centre without other help. He will still be interacting with the process in a way that should help to clarify his needs. The design of the service should help this to happen. Generally, however, it is likely that a person (whom we describe later and generically as a consultant) will be brought into the process. The advantage of this is that it helps to 'externalise' the ideas the enquirer has in mind. If the enquirer is a teacher, this can be of great help, since ultimately he has to bring out his statements for the pupil. The librarian or producer can in these circumstances act as a substitute for the pupil and help the teacher see whether his approach is a satisfactory one. Ultimately the teacher has something of a consultant's role himself in his relationship with the pupil, with whom it is now his turn to clarify the argument.

There is another important advantage to be derived from these discussions about books and materials. They tend to provide an opportunity for a neutral discussion on a teacher's method. Insofar as a teacher's methods of communication are based on talking with pupils, it is extremely difficult for anyone else to discuss them with him. It is an intensely personal process and it can easily be understood why teachers have carefully guarded their privacy. (Microteaching attempts to invade this privacy but it is not universally accepted as a useful method.) If, however, we discuss the needs of the teacher for books, materials or new productions, we focus on these and depersonalise the process. As in team teaching, an environment is created in which the teacher's methods can be discussed but implicitly rather than explicitly. The sense of this seems to derive from the fact that both persons are looking together at a third object rather than looking at each other in a somewhat critical sense. The participants may not even be consciously aware of this but experience suggests that in the best kind of discussion this is what is happening.

Again, in such a discussion the ambivalence of communication is manifest. We make certain statements to each other and tend to focus upon these as the substance of the communication. However, it is often the case that our apparent disagreement derives not from the statements which we are exchanging, but from the fact that we are making them from within a different context. It is these contexts which we need to explore, and the suggestion here is that the librarian, resource officer or producer is well suited to help the teacher (or pupil) carry out the exploration, and prepare him for the fact that the person to whom he conveys the information will certainly feel a need to identify the context from within which he is addressing them. It is easy to identify the facts we exchange, but this must not be allowed to disguise from us the fact that it is the context within which we use them that creates our differences, and that these contexts are much more difficult to determine. It should be the aim of any communicator to simplify the argument so that both the information and the structure can be understood: to omit all that is unnecessary but to retain all that is essential.

Throughout this section we have tried to demonstrate the relationship between form and content, and we have suggested that using different forms of presentation enhances our understanding. Experience suggests that the librarian, resource officer, or producer should be primarily concerned to promote this process and help his enquirers place their need for information in a new context. If, as Richards says, 'meanings mind their company', we can help the enquirer to provide a variety of company for his meanings, in order the better to understand them.

CHAPTER III

Function in practice

So far we have considered communication in a rather theoretical mode. How does this affect the workings of a library, resource centre or audiovisual unit?

First we must define what are here seen to be the functions of these three organisations. The library began as a collection of printed materials brought together so that the user could more easily have access to them. However, it became evident, particularly in more recent years, that users were often ill-equipped to make the best use of the resources offered to them, and they could benefit considerably from assistance, provided to give them a better understanding of the contents and organisation of the collection. The reference librarian, and later the information officer, was born. It is the thesis of this book that this intermediate, or consultancy role of the librarian is his most important function. Users need and should be given help in relating their questions and problems to the collection of books which they intend to consult. The benefit they derive from this is not only a better chance of finding the answer they seek, but probably of finding a better question in the context of the problem they are pursuing. The librarian, by relating the possibilities of his collection to the user's problem, gives the user a wider insight into that problem and does not just provide the extra information that at first sight may seem to be all that is necessary.

The organiser of a resource collection has precisely the same role as a librarian. He, too, has a collection of materials brought together so that a user can have easier access to them and he, too, can help the user by discussing his questions in relation to the nature of the collection.

It is perhaps less obvious that an audiovisual unit also serves the same purpose. Indeed, since it is concerned almost wholly with the presentation of information, it can become an even more powerful influence to help reorganise ideas than perhaps a library.

An audiovisual unit consists essentially of the means of making materials. They may be quite simple such as duplicating machines, photocopying devices and off-air recording systems. They may be complex with sophisticated television studios and photographic units. But primarily they offer the means of producing materials. However, although they have usually been set up for this purpose, it is becoming increasingly clear that the actual production of materials is not necessarily the most important part of their function. Much more important are the process of making the material, and the effect this process has on the people involved, whether they be teachers or students. As soon as somebody considers the possibility of making or having made any kind of material, he has immediately to consider his subject matter in the context of this form of presentation. This, like the enquiry at the reference or information desk in the library, very easily leads him into a different type of examination of his subject and hence possibly to an enhanced understanding.

It is, again, the thesis of this book, that this reconsideration of one's subject is the most important factor in the use of audiovisual materials, and not the additional information that they may provide. Indeed, it might be argued that, generally speaking, they are rather inadequate for providing information, and that their strength lies in the provision of different interpretations of basically the same information.

The user of audiovisual materials will come under the influence of this reconsideration even if he works with them entirely on his own. Putting together the simplest tape/slide programme will force him into a serious reconsideration of his subject unless he is totally insensitive to the inconsistencies he will otherwise certainly produce. However, if he is able to work with a producer, or media consultant who is professionally qualified in presentation techniques, the ensuing discussion will provide even more insight into the nature of the subject and the problems which arise in its presentation. As with the discussion with the librarian, the user will gain additional insights into his subject matter. This will arise whether the producer is making the material for the user or advising him on how to make it himself.

It seems appropriate to describe this function of librarian or producer as a consultancy. In both cases they are acting as catalysts to facilitate the reaction between the user and the resources at his disposal.

Now it is clear that not every request of a library or audiovisual unit will require the personal intervention of a member of staff. If the user knows exactly which book he requires it must be possible for him to go to a catalogue and then find it on the shelves; if someone wants a simple photocopy made he should either be able to do it himself or hand it in via some simple system to have it done. In effect, however, these are requests for information or service which occur sufficiently often and with a repetitive pattern for the 'consultant' to establish a routine procedure.

In designing these procedures the consultant is selecting those enquiries which arise so frequently that they can be systematised, and the procedure becomes a routine service. Its dominant characteristic is its structure, insofar as someone approaching it with a query can be directed to the right point of entry, and he will then be taken through the system in such a way that his needs are met. The crucial condition here is that the person is directed to the right point of entry. This assumes that the unit has clearly identified for the user where the point of entry is for different services, and just what the service is which that point of entry provides. It is also necessary for the user to be able to recognise his request in the terms in which the unit identifies its services.

The number of users who get themselves lost at service points indicates that this is a very important problem. It arises from the fact we have referred to above, that although the point of entry is the common physical contact between the user and the unit, each looks upon this clearly defined fact in quite a different context. The unit sees it as the focal point for a large range of resources: the user sees it as the focal point for a large range of questions. These two concepts need to be brought together, and this must be achieved within the mind of the user, who is the only person to whom the interrelationship is significant. The unit must therefore provide its points of entry so that each customer comes to recognise them also as his points of entry.

An immediate difficulty here presents itself. The unit is clearly being asked to meet the needs of each individual user, whatever his special interest may be. This is clearly uneconomic, and the unit must itself determine the point of entry to its system beyond which it cannot afford to go. It must then explicitly or implicitly make this clear to users. The user is then faced with a point of entry which may appear to be far from that at which he would like to come in. This is a frequent cause of complaint and confusion. Many unit managers, whether librarians, or producers, feel they must at all costs meet all possible demands. This is particularly the case with indexes. Everything in a collection must be indexed under every relevant heading.

The alternative is to admit that there is a possible extra point of entry to the system, but you the consultant deemed it unjustifiable to provide it. Given that the irate user in front of you naturally thinks his need is supreme amongst everyone else's, this is an admission that requires a certain amount of toughness on the part of the unit manager! Even greater toughness is perhaps required if we take the user to the next stage in the relationship between him and the unit.

If he does not find a convenient point of entry to the system, there is a discontinuity between what the user wants and what the unit provides. Is this to be treated as a gap in the services which must be filled, or is it to be a space in which there can be a discussion which we hope will enable both user and service to determine a fruitful point of contact? It is the job of the consultant to decide, and either provide an extended routine service or facilitate the discussion. The discussion may take place at the simplest level, for not all of this occurs in a remote intellectual climate. The user may want an ABC timetable, and the librarian (in this case) may have to persuade him to use a British Rail one. Alternatively, he may want a tape/slide presentation of a script which he has written, which the producer (in this case) will decide is quite unsuitable in style. The difficulties of communication between the consultant on the one hand and user on the other are fundamentally the same in each case, although perhaps of a different order of magnitude. Many people will avoid using anything but an ABC timetable since this is laid out so simply. They will need a lot of encouragement to accept the alternative and more complicated one. In the case of the tape-slide, the user may well feel his cherished ideas are being totally neglected by the producer, and yet the significance of the producer's ideas will only become evident when he has finished his version. Consequently there is need of a great degree of confidence by the user that the producer has in fact understood his problem and is going to produce something which will work according to his ideas. If there is this confidence, and it should, of course, grow as they experience working together, then a presentation will result to which they have both contributed. The differences between them will have created a new product which includes the best of each. It is often not appreciated that it is only because of the differences between two approaches that we can have a fruitful discussion which will clarify both views. If there are no differences between two people, then it is extremely difficult for them to have a discussion, fruitful or otherwise.

Let us take this concept of the creativity of differences a little further since an appreciation of it should underline all of the work of a consultant in a resource centre, whatever its nature. When we formulate a problem, or a question which we think a library or audiovisual unit will help us with, we can only proceed as far as our own understanding of the problem allows. We follow the paths and byways of our conception of the subject, our own structure, until we come to a barred gate beyond which we find ourselves unable to pass. At that point we seek help in opening the gate, and it may be we discover that the unit possesses only the key to an altogether different gate. If we function unimaginatively, no progress seems possible and there is no further contact. However, to continue the metaphor, there are nearly always other routes to any destination, although they may not be easy to find. If the user steps back from his gate and formulates his need in more general terms, the unit may find that, seen from a distance, their best help is not to provide the key they first offered, but perhaps to provide a map of alternatives. The important point is that by using the map the user may well find not only an alternative to the gate he first identified, but what proves to be a much better route altogether. It is often the case that a unit's inability to answer the question first put to it, far from baulking the user may, if he is given suitable assistance, stimulate him to a much more fruitful approach.

This is, of course, a frequent form of discussion with children, who are prone to ask the first question that comes into their heads. More often than not the parent or teacher can, by a judicious series of questions, help the child to answer his own question from his own knowledge and understanding. This can even happen with adults, but in their case the difficulty often lies in their inability to accept that any other question at all may be useful, or even better than the one they first thought of. So often when we pose a question we fail to determine its precise impact on our future action. How accurately do we need to have the answer?

How will our behaviour be affected if we do not answer the question? Can we proceed without an answer, providing we retain a mental note that we may need to come back for one? As we proceed we may find the significance of the question recedes and we no longer need to answer it. Or it may become of increasing importance and we need to know even more precisely. It is not the answers we obtain which are important, but rather the questions we formulate in the first place.

Education is a field of study in which people are particularly prone uselessly and dangerously to seek perfect answers. Uselessly because perfect answers are not to be found; dangerously because we are discouraged from working with less than perfect answers, with an awareness that they are less than perfect but may nevertheless generate better questions. It is surely an important function of education that it should train us to be able to live with this kind of uncertainty.

It is not unusual to find educational experts talking in such terms as finding the 'most effective way of teaching reading'. This implies that there is a way which will far exceed all others in the number of readers it will produce. One would have thought that the number of schemes already in existence would have demonstrated the impossibility of perfecting one method, but such facts do not seem to inhibit speakers in these terms. They seem completely to overlook the complex personal processes involved in an activity like reading, or indeed any other learning process. Apart from skills involving our eyes and our perception, our emotions and our feelings also determine whether we learn and what we learn. These will sometimes respond to one approach and sometimes to another. Sometimes we want cake and sometimes we want bread, and it is stupid to argue that one or the other is the right way to obtain nourishment.

The most effective way to teach something will be the method to which the learner responds at that time. It will be the teacher's responsibility to decide which method to use in the light of the situation in which he finds himself. (It might also be seen as part of the teacher's job to help students ultimately to determine for themselves how best they could learn something.) Although certain attributes of any scheme may be helpful in deciding that it is appropriate in a given situation, the teacher must eventually make a judgment, which in advance will not be provable, that a particular scheme is appropriate. We will seldom be able to define in advance the circumstances in which a student will succeed, but we will have no difficulty in recognising whether or not he has succeeded. It is extremely important that in education (as a process of communication) we should be willing to use our instinctive judgment even when we have no tangible reason to expect it to work. We must live with the uncertainty and see what happens.

It is surely significant that so often in fairy tales, from all countries, the hero is told by some good fairy to take a journey which will lead him to what he wants. When the hero asks how he will know when he has got there he is told this cannot be vouchsafed to him, but that he will know when he finds it that it is what he seeks. What a splendid guide to teachers that represents! We should not seek to find the 'most effective way to teach reading', but rather awaken in teachers an awareness of the problems they are likely to come across and offer them a range of methods for dealing with them. They will not be guaranteed success, but they will certainly recognise it when they achieve it.

A search for panaceas is all too common in society and in education. We search for them in vain, for we cannot predict the circumstances in which they will be needed. Failure with all methods can be guaranteed at some time or another, and we must face this fact and be confident in the use of alternative approaches. If the gate is shut, look at the map for other exits. We must therefore provide good maps. That is the function of the staff of a library, or a production unit, and particularly of the person with the closest contact with the student, the teacher.

CHAPTER IV

Organisation

With the coming of new kinds of materials in considerable quantities there has been much argument over where they should be housed, and how they should be handled. In addition, the production facilities for the new materials give rise to many discussions on their best location. The hinge of the discussions has been the library. The argument usually resolves itself into whether 'non-book materials' and their means of production should or should not form part of the library, whether it be in a school, college or university. It is of interest that the problem seems to be less serious in public libraries, which readily handle gramophone records, tapes, prints, archives, manuscripts and so on. Indeed, it is possible that many of the difficulties with the new resources arise from the quite extraordinary attitude, common until recently, and still not unknown, adopted by teachers towards libraries.

At first sight it would seem to be obvious that the educational process just could not proceed without access to past knowledge. Indeed teachers spend a great deal of their time conveying just that. But in doing so some seem quite oblivious of the value of the records of past knowledge to be found in a library. One headmistress once agreed that children could consult books in the school library provided they did not go beyond a certain shelf, 'otherwise they would have nothing to read next year'. Yet the same person declined an offer of assistance from the local childrens' librarian as she 'felt the school had all the books it needed'. To this headmistress the idea seemed completely foreign that books were the means by which the childrens' minds could be fertilised and nourished, the better to cultivate the knowledge and enthusiasm the teacher can impart. Surely there is no child who will not be stimulated somehow by some book because of its content, or its design, or its illustrations. And if illustrations are a recognised resource in a book, can we logically justify their separation into a different collection? Fortunately, the idea of combining book libraries, media collections, and media production gains ground, but the fact that the argument has arisen is surely a disturbing reflection of the attitude to learning of many librarians and teachers.

This chapter considers the problems which arise in the organisation and administration of materials from a common standpoint, for whether we consider a media or an audiovisual unit, a library or a resource centre there are common functions to be performed.

We have already suggested that the first of these may be regarded generically as consultancy. This function is to guide the user so that his enquiry can be organised in the way that most suits the resources available. It is a truism that a person hardly ever asks precisely the question to which he really wants the reply. This is basically because his problem will seldom be susceptible only to a single answer. Unfortunately, we all of us have a tendency to behave as if this is not the case, and accordingly object if the source of the desired answer is not available. Yet, few questions cannot be enlarged upon or clarified with advantage. It therefore behoves us, when approaching a resource centre of any kind, to keep an open mind about how it is going to assist us.

We may think of ourselves as having a framework in our minds made up of certain information which is associated by our experience (and personality) to form a pattern of some sort. It has some gaps or open ends, and these constitute our questions. We may think that only one question is relevant at a particular time, but if the idea of a pattern is accepted it will be evident that it is most unlikely that it can only be developed, or that a gap can only be filled, by the answer to one particular question. A quite different question may evoke an answer which closes a gap in such a way that the original question is superseded. A visual analogy is the way in which the sea, on an incoming tide, flows round obstacles and fills the small gullies until an obstacle is itself suddenly overwhelmed.

As we approach a resource system of any kind we should try and see how we can infiltrate it, so that even if it appears at first sight not to be able to help us, we may be able to find other questions to which it does indeed contain the answers.

If we are familiar with the resources, we may be able to exploit them effectively without further assistance. However, if we are to do so, someone will have had to organise them and this defines the first person we need on the staff. He needs to be able to foresee the real needs of users and interrelate them with the facilities he has at his disposal. Further, he needs to be able to signpost the facilities so that the user will be able to exploit them to the full; or if the user comes to a point of doubt, he must be directed to the person who will, by person-to-person discussion, be able to move the relationship between the problem and the resources forward once more. It is this planning role that is performed by the consultant.

We may now consider the consultant's rôle more precisely in terms of the different kinds of media organisation.

Let us consider first the organisation of a collection of media. The consultant will be what we normally know as a librarian. Many times, of course, such a person is asked where a particular item is located, or for information of a clearly defined nature. He will, hopefully, direct the enquirer, but he should also consider whether he should provide better directions which would have allowed the user to find his own way.

Then there are those questions which have clearly been thought out, and perhaps developed to match the collection. The enquirer may here be thought to have looked at his problem through a library filter, and come to those questions which arise from the interaction of the problem and the filter. But it is most unlikely that these questions will exhaust all the possibilities of the interaction. It is the consultant's job to examine this situation and discover what other associations can be established between the enquiry and the materials which he has at his disposal.

Given this description of the basis of the librarian's work, it will be evident that it extends automatically into other media than books, and that the separation of materials into books handled by librarians and non-books handled by others is meaningless. All the materials we are discussing contain information. Different materials structure the same information in different ways, but this merely means that they complement each other and thus can enhance our understanding of the information they contain. The exploitation of a collection of books and non-books requires the same skill from the organiser.

If we turn to the organisation of media production we can see that the same considerations apply. The librarian helps the enquirer to structure his information and his questions so that they can be related to the resources available. A consultant in an audio visual unit also helps the enquirer to structure his information so that it can be related to the resources available—only now the resources are the different forms of physical presentation.

Let us consider a simple example. Reprographic facilities exist to make overhead transparencies. How can the enquirer be helped to organise his material so that it can be successfully converted into this media-form? It is likely that he will be expecting either too many transparencies to be shown in the time available, or too much information to be carried in each transparency for it to be assimilable. The consultant here must raise those questions to which the answers enable him to design transparencies containing no more information than can be seen and comprehended by the viewer, and in numbers which extend to match the time available. The same process takes place as with a question for a library. In order to match the enquiry with the resources, it must be restructured, and the restructuring process will add to the understanding of the enquirer.

The relationship between the consultant (*ie* librarian or producer) and the user is a creative one, adding ideas, or structures, which may not have been evident to the enquirer in the first place. Yet the information which he has will not necessarily have changed; his understanding of it will. It is a familiar experience that writing an article, giving a lecture, preparing a film or television programme, even on a very familiar topic, tests the imagination and twists the ideas so that the subject matter becomes that much more deeply ingrained in the mind. The consultant's role, whether in the library or the media unit, is to facilitate this process.

A consultant, however, cannot function in isolation. First, he requires technical skills to be available so that he can function effectively. In a library he needs cataloguers and classifiers and purchasers. Their function is to produce the material and organise it for access. Similarly, in a production unit there are technicians, engineers, photographers, graphic designers, whose job is to produce the material and, in effect, organise it, or design it.

We have here spoken as though the tasks outlined for consultants and technicians are totally separate. As functions they are, but as tasks they may well be carried out by the same person. In a large unit they may be separated by reason of the number of staff involved; in a small unit it may well be the same person who carries out both sets of tasks.

Even if they are the work of different people, the nature of the relationship between them and the user may have overlapping qualities. The cataloguer and classifier who does not appreciate the needs of the user is likely to be wasting many of the resources he organises. He must know the pattern of use of the collection he is serving and relate new additions to this pattern. Similarly, the graphic designer must identify with the needs of his user to produce materials which are in a style appropriate to the use that will be made of them. And to be aware of style is to come very close to the role of the consultant, for both require a sense of structure and pattern, or environment within which the exchange of ideas will take place.

Finally we have the clerical staff necessary to maintain records of acquisitions and borrowings, to programme production work, to make external exchanges and to keep accounts. Much of this work may be of an entirely predetermined nature, but even at its most mundane level it is likely to demand some initiative—for example, when to pursue an item, and when it is reasonable not to do so. Once again it is a question of matching the need to the resources, and questioning whether a particular activity will strengthen the work, or whether it represents a waste of effort. A decision will be necessary on the basis of judgment rather than facts. The dilemma we referred to in chapter 1 manifests itself at all levels. How important it is, then, that we should train our students to realise this!

Questions are frequently raised about the type of staff required, particularly for resource centres and school libraries, and these are considered further in the next chapter. However, in this context we should consider an issue that often arises—whether or not to centralise resources. Frequently this can be not an administrative issue, but a personal one. Mr X has taken the initiative to order a piece of equipment, or a set of books, and is very reluctant to allow anyone else (whom he privately, or sometimes publicly, believes would be incapable of using it) to have access to it. The resolution of such problems comes rather in a manual of management. Here we can only consider the ideal.

Certain principles apply. First, resources should be used to the maximum. Second, they should be used efficiently. Here we have another dilemma, for if they are to be used to the maximum it is likely that they will be located with the group who have most need of them or know most about them. On the other hand this may well prevent other groups from gaining access. If they are to be used efficiently they may require specialist handling, either in the operation of equipment, or the utilisation of materials. The specialist may already be present in a department, or he may be specially recruited for a central post.

Cost is ultimately the deciding factor, and this must be judged, not in absolute terms, but in terms of the relative cost to the institution. Ideally, basic materials and equipment should be readily available to different groups. Thus a simple slide projector might be installed in every classroom, and, similarly, a basic collection of books. On the other hand, a videotape recorder is likely to be held in a central unit, as will the major collection of reference books. The argument is not, as it so often seems to be expressed, about the rightness of classroom libraries against a central library, but solely one of finance.

A related issue which affects large organisations is whether or not to charge for the use of production facilities. Unless a section or an individual has a separate budget, the question does not, of course, arise. Where there is a separate budget it can be argued that the customer might be expected to pay for the cost of materials. In this way only a minimum amount of money needs to be allocated to materials from the central budget, and it is possible for a more specific control to be exercised on expenditure.

On the other hand, if it is necessary to encourage the use of materials in a perhaps reluctant community, the imposition of a charge may have an inhibiting effect, whereas free materials out of central funds may stimulate an interest. However, there is then the danger that so much material is used that the production budget rises out of all proportion to other expenditure; that is probably the time to institute some form of local charging for materials.

The facilities which are necessary to produce the materials should always be a charge on central funds. Otherwise it will be impossible to maintain a continuity of staffing and equipment, nor will it be possible to ensure that they are always equally available to everyone.

As a footnote to this chapter, my colleague Peter Morris has put forward an analysis of the role of the graphic designer in education which seems to give a useful insight into the work of what he describes as 'intermediary units', *ie* libraries, resource centres, production units. In his view, the graphic designer functions at three levels:

Level 1 —collaboration on course design, learning methods, integration of materials and objectives; teaching.

Level 2 —development of materials where understanding of subject and teaching objectives is important.

Level 3 —routine graphic design service where no subject or specialist knowledge is required.

As we have suggested earlier in the chapter, it does not follow that a different person functions at each level. Often the same person will operate at more than one level, but it is perhaps helpful to recognise that he will be performing one or more of these roles. It does seem that we are better able to cooperate with each other if we have a clear idea of our respective roles.

Turning to librarians it would seem possible to extend to their work the three levels set out above. Librarians could certainly take part in course design, bringing to bear their knowledge of existing materials and, perhaps most important, how students use them. Where courses already exist, librarians can compile reading lists and bibliographies, and put together special collections. Finally, they can provide a routine service based on the normal library procedures.

This analysis can be correlated with that given in the text. Level 1 is pure consultancy; level 2 is consultancy with some technical content; and level 3 is wholly technical. The correlation is particularly interesting, since graphic design courses seem increasingly to be sources of staff for media collections and resource centres.

CHAPTER V

Staff

'If you are not understood, seek to understand him who did not understand you and to know why he did not'*
In any resource service the rôle of the staff is paramount. Their attitudes and actions effectively determine whether the resources they control will be used to the best advantage or not. This is true whether or not they always have direct contact with the user. Many of the facilities will be designed for the user to apply himself: copying machines, recorders, catalogues and the materials themselves may all be available for the user without any need for him to contact a member of staff.

Nevertheless, the way in which these services are organised, the instructions given for their use, the decisions taken to provide such a service on a direct basis for the user, all require an understanding of the user's problem and, even more important, an understanding of the way he approaches it. Staff therefore are the most important element in a resource area. Indeed, one can probably say that the services offered should be geared to the staff available, and if staff cannot be found with the requisite skills for a particular style of service this should not be attempted.

This view is particularly important at the creative level. Part of the user's skill in exploiting a resource service, and of the consultant's skill as well, lies in developing a request so that it will lie within the interests, abilities and enthusiasms of the staff.

* Tierno Bokar (Mali), quoted from Sabena Revue 1974, no 1, Brussels, p 14.

We have suggested in the previous chapter that the staff of a centre will fall into three categories—consultants, technicians and clerks—and we may for convenience summarise their functions.

Consultants are the organisers. Their basic function is to build the bridge between the user's needs and the resources available to meet them. They organise the centre, they organise its resources (both materials and equipment), they organise the approach to the resources and, tactfully, they organise the user so that his problem can be matched to the facilities available.

Technicians provide the machinery on which the organisation runs. They may be thought of as 'engineers', since they engineer the process and ensure that it runs smoothly for the user. The machinery of the system may be physical plant in the form of audiovisual equipment, or it may be a television service, but it can also be the catalogue of a library and the filing cabinets and shelves for the collection.

Clerks provide the essential paperwork for the system. Documentation in all its forms is necessary if materials and services are to flow smoothly.

It is clearly wrong to suggest that this exact separation of functions exists in reality. They obviously overlap in execution, and it will be one of the purposes of this chapter to emphasise this point. But even if the functions overlap within one person, it is still valid to distinguish between functions. Let us consider them in more detail.

Roderick MacLean, Director of Audio-Visual Services at Glasgow and Strathclyde Universities has discussed the qualifications needed in producers (*ie* in our terms, media consultants) in the audiovisual centre. He considers the producer from three aspects: role, qualifications and personality.

The role of a producer is fourfold. He protects the teacher from the medium; he provides an inclusive knowledge of media; he determines the style, suitability and choice of material; and organises, manages and coordinates.

The qualifications of the producer are first grounded in media, and should include practical as well as examination qualifications; he needs to have some understanding of psychology, in particular motivation and perception; he needs some knowledge of teaching methods (but not so that he can practise), and he must have a grasp of language.

The personality of a producer must enable him to play the part of an audience; he must be forthright, objective and, most important, an acceptable critic; he must mix confidence with professional diffidence.

If we now apply this analysis to the work of a librarian as a consultant in his field there is seen to be a very close correlation.

The librarian, like the producer, protects the user from the medium (*ie* he arranges, say, 500,000 books so that the user can find what he wants); he provides an inclusive knowledge of media (*ie* he knows his way round bibliographies, abstracts, other libraries, resources); he determines the style, suitability and choice of material (*ie* he is responsible for the build-up of the collection); he organises, manages and coordinates (*ie* he does just that).

The producer must be qualified in media, the librarian in librarianship. He needs to have some understanding of psychology and a knowledge of teaching methods; for the librarian precisely so. Finally, he must have a grasp of language—and so should any librarian worth his salt.

The personality of the librarian must enable him to become an audience—certainly when listening to the user's enquiry or envisaging a user's enquiry. He must be forthright, objective and an acceptable critic; this is certainly necessary in a reader's adviser, and in the designer of library systems, whose job will necessarily require something of the reader which he may not be prepared to volunteer. He must mix confidence with professional diffidence—an admirable recipe for any professional.

It seems, **there**fore, that, certainly insofar as attitude of mind is concerned, there is a great deal in common between the producer and the librarian. If they accept this, then surely they can live together under the same roof. It requires of them a respect for each other's professional skill (confidence with professional diffidence), and a readiness to decide how best to utilise the different skills that they respectively make available. Insofar as they are both interested in exploiting resources and adapting requests to the resources available, then if they are successful in this they should be able to adapt to each other. In other words, if the organiser, under whatever hat he functions, understands the problem of exploiting resources, then there is certainly justification for amalgamating libraries, resource centres and audiovisual units.

On the other hand, it is not the purpose of this book to suggest that we should seek to train multipurpose individuals who could both produce a television programme and run a branch library. Clearly some such people exist and they will have much to contribute to our work in this field, but they are few. What we have endeavoured to show is that there is a common philosophy underlying the work of libraries and audiovisual units, and that it is at this level of understanding that a common link ought to be established between producers and librarians. Within that understanding there is need for different kinds of experience and different qualifications, but they must complement each other and recognise the sense of common purpose which should motivate them.

In small organisations such as a school, circumstances often force a combination of roles, since so few staff are available. Even then it is useful to recognise that one person is encompassing a number of different functions, but important to realise that these multiple roles are not fundamentally in conflict, although their implementation may produce practical difficulties. In larger organisations it should be possible to employ enough staff to organise separate units. It is, however, impossible to conceive arguments which would justify the provision of literal answers to queries in one place, and visual answers in another. It is equally difficult to justify sending the user to one place if the visual answer already exists, and to another place if it has to be prepared. His initial contact with any section of the information service should clearly elicit his need, even though he may then require the application of different skills to answer it.

In universities and polytechnics the library has the traditional role of providing authoritative texts and up-to-date printed information across the disciplines taught, but in many subjects it is now recognised that visual and aural materials are sources of comparable standing. Significant in this respect is the growing interest of historians in film records.[10] Also in university and polytechnic libraries, as the emphasis shifts to the provision of services to support teaching programmes, the concept of a resource centre, itself supported by a production unit, becomes more important and can be seen as a natural development of library service. The process of extension will not occur overnight. Staff will need to live with a gradual rate of change and development. But if the target is set, then within a measurable period of time it is possible to achieve an integrated service.

An important problem which faces many institutions attempting to set up integrated services is how to find the staff for such a service. Librarians have a well organised career structure and, broadly speaking, a training programme which matches it. Audio-visual producers have a much more recent history, and only within the last few years since their incorporation into education has the question of a career structure arisen. Gradually as more units are set up it is becoming possible for a career structure for producers to be identified. At the same time attempts are being made to establish the training needs for such posts, but these can only be tentative in the present stage of development. Producers, unless they come from broadcasting corporations, tend to be taught on the job with no clearly defined pattern of training. It can therefore be difficult for a librarian, needing a producer, to know where to find such a person and what qualifications to ask for. Graphic design courses, in fact, seem to provide a sound background for this work when they are broad enough to include all media. Some colleges are now developing graphic design courses with the needs of education particularly in mind. But it could well be that the original broad course offered a better background for an understanding of educational needs, which could then best be gained on the job.

Undoubtedly the establishment of integrated units raises difficulties, because we are trying to blend the skills of two professions which do not automatically accept that they have a common purpose. It is true that if the members of each think of themselves as offering a service which the user asks for, their functions will scarcely overlap. But as soon as they appreciate the opportunity they have to develop the user's questions and become involved in his problems then an identity of interest becomes self-evident.

One of the difficulties is that we are all habitually slow to learn to utilise resources—which in this particular case are the skills of our professional colleagues. We have already commented that some teachers manage to function in spite of the infrequent use that most of them make of a local or school library. They seem to lack the interest which would make them want to exploit resources, and, even more, to train pupils to do so. We must, however, recognise that teachers are not alone in this, although it may be more reprehensible in their profession. We are all, including librarians and media consultants, reluctant to change our habits, or to adopt new methods.

We must recognise that the employment of new resources will do more than just add to the range of activities. It will almost certainly lead on to changes in the pattern of work and in the approach to work. This will not only affect the user of the resources, whether he be teacher or student, but will also affect us, the organisers of the resources. This is the difficulty and the challenge for librarians and producers. Whilst both librarians and media producers must maintain their professional standards, they must also be ready to develop and adapt them in collaboration with each other. And, as the user learns from his interaction with the resources, so the librarian and media producer should learn more about their own professions from their interaction with each other.

We now turn to the second staff group, technicians. The equation of librarians with technicians may create umbrage, but let us consider the context within which the phrase is being used.

First it is important to emphasise the *creative* role of a technician. It is certainly not his function blindly to apply the most sophisticated techniques at his disposal. He must, like the producer, adapt each system to the demands placed upon it, and realise and suggest how they might be better met with the facilities at his disposal. Thus, in a sound amplifier a frequency response of equal value from 5 to 50,000 cycles may be necessary for a lecturer demonstrating the varying response to sound of the human ear as it ages. For music a response is required which matches the sensitivity of the particular audience. But for ordinary speech almost any type of frequency response is adequate. Similar variations in demand levels apply to other equipment in the unit.

As a parallel of a kind, the cataloguer of a special university collection is obliged to prepare the most detailed entry for each item, even if it takes several months to complete the catalogue. In a large public reference library, a more limited description of each text will probably suffice, and in a small collection of books in a primary school it may not be necessary to have a catalogue at all, since 99% of the readership will always go straight to the shelves, and the effort required to serve the remaining 1% will be unjustified.

The master of a technique puts his knowledge (*ie* structured information) at the disposal of a user in order best to meet the latter's needs. A multiplicity of detail, whether it relates to cataloguing, classification, adjustments on projectors or tape-recorders, can only be justified if the user would not be satisfied with less. There is a difficulty, however. The measure of the user's satisfaction must be taken by him and the technician together, for the user alone is unable to assess how useful extra technical help would be. This is also very difficult for a technician to judge. He will know how the technique could be refined and how the user would benefit as a consequence, and yet if he does not restrain himself he may pile complication on complication. He must stop short when he knows that at the technical level he could still do better. One of the most important qualifications to be sought in this grade of post is the ability to make such judgments. Too much complication confuses the user. Too little means he is not as well served as he could be. The decision must rest with the technician.

When we consider the necessary qualifications of people who will be employed in these posts, it is clear that at technician level there is less opportunity for interchange of roles as between libraries and media units. In the organisation of materials we need cataloguers and classifiers, people who, in general, will still be learning the library profession as a whole, and if the organisation is a large one, there will be room for senior and experienced librarians who have chosen to specialise in these fields. For the production of graphic materials we may look to designers, probably with qualifications in art and graphic design or an equivalent. Equipment specialists, on the other hand, may well be radio or television engineers, or electronics engineers by training.

As with producers, media technicians constitute a new staff category, which in turn establishes new relationships between existing disciplines. There is some scope for informal interchange of activities in new and small units, of course. It may be that a school, developing for historical reasons a media centre rather than a library, will employ in the first place a graphic designer, who then develops an aptitude for helping pupils find information from books and other sources; he or she may then begin to organise a collection of materials—in fact, to develop a library. Eventually, this side of the work grows to justify the appointment of a librarian, and the two professionals should be able to work in harmony.

Alternatively, the growth may be from a school library in

which the 'orthodox' librarian has a firm sense of style and presentation, so that he or she can contribute to the design of new materials until such time as a graphic designer may be required. The approach described here is manifest in the posts of Media Resource Officers within the Inner London Education Authority. The backgrounds of most persons currently filling these posts are far more diverse than has been suggested here, yet they are all fulfilling a similar function.

The training of personnel to carry out a multiple role is difficult and it is perhpas significant that the ILEA have found it necessary to design their own special courses for MROs. The City and Guilds of London Institute has also designed an audiovisual course which covers design, photography, electronics and physics, but this is almost too general to be of direct use. Specialist courses raise fewer problems. Cataloguers and classifiers derive their training as part of a general librarianship course, although it is perhaps unfortunate that part-time courses no longer exist for mature students to follow, whilst working or for teachers and media specialists to gain some experience. Designers normally have also taken a full-time course, although there are some related part-time courses. Engineers generally have easy access to a variety of college courses which assume that working experience is available as part of the training process.

The problem of the relationship between professions is never going to be fully resolved. There will always be arguments and disagreements. Nevertheless we must not forget that the professional places himself at the service of his community, and whilst on the one hand it is right that he should protect the status of his profession, it is vital, if we are to exploit our professional resources, that we should recognise the overlap that is often present and have the patience to see whether this may not be the seed from which a new profession will grow.

Finally we turn to clerical staff. In a large organisation they function behind the scenes, backing up the work of the other staff. Normal, but various qualifications apply. In small organisations the clerical staff may be out in front dealing with user enquiries, while the technical and organisation staff are working on other projects. In cases where there are only one or two staff, the work of the unit may revolve round the 'secretary', and the way in which she coordinates the customers' needs with the resources available.

Such key, 'non-denominational' figures are already known in small libraries and media units. They provide a basic common-sense guide to the collection, they invariably lack any professional qualifications, and yet are often the lynch-pin of the service. They have acquired the ability to understand what the customer wants, and even in cases where there is no clear understanding, produce an experienced awareness of how the problem can be resolved. In some ways it is a true secretarial role, superintending the flow of work—the description 'secretary' has been debased by the need to inflate the status of shorthand typists. Appointments in this group depend perhaps more than in any other on personality, since the measurable skills are limited. Typing, perhaps shorthand, orderliness with papers, but most important of all, the right look in the eye which makes users want to expound their needs and be encouraged to return to the unit for further help.

CHAPTER VI

Facilities

This chapter is mainly concerned with the design of an audiovisual unit and the production facilities with which it needs to be supplied. The storage and arrangement of materials, which is the normal library function, is dealt with in the next chapter.

The most important facility for the production of materials is space. By this is not necessarily meant large areas, though, clearly, the more space, the better. Even more important is it that the available space should be open and uncluttered, and therefore permit flexibility of use. On the whole, an open space of not less than 150 square feet is the minimum useful area. If more than, say, 300 square feet are available, it is probably best to subdivide the area into smaller units. In addition, peripheral working surfaces are needed, which can most economically be provided by workbenches set around the walls with storage cupboards beneath. This kind of surface intrudes very little into the room and yet provides a good area to lay out materials. The storage space is essential. Free-standing units involve the minimum of fixing, and if it is desired to alter the arrangement at any time, they can be moved without difficulty. The benches must be a comfortable height for working, either when standing or seated on a stool, and should be 2–3 feet deep. A plastic finish gives a smart appearance, which encourages good housekeeping and is easier to keep clean.

Production facilities are, in fact, conventional studio facilities, as for a design studio with drawing boards, a photographic studio with space for installing backcloth and lights, a film or television studio suitable at least for simple portable equipment. If the requirement is primarily for reprographic equipment, this can be accommodated on the working space. If the unit is ambitious in its scope, several of the different activities may be undertaken in rotation, which emphasises the need in a single studio for flexibility in layout and adequate storage space.

We now turn to some of the principles of equipment. This first difficulty is that there are so many different manufacturers to choose from. By and large, it makes sense to assume that reliability is a fairly constant factor and that, like the modern motor car, one model is as prone to breakdown as another. Similarly, most large organisations still do not know how to organise a reliable maintenance and repair service, so purchases must be made with this in mind. Many suppliers offer substantial discounts which may tempt education authorities with limited budgets, but when the equipment goes wrong, and it certainly will do, service will be required and quickly. Discounts are often at the expense of after-sales service.

Reliability is an important quality in all equipment, and is most likely to be present when the equipment is simple to operate. Automatic equipment of any kind has incorporated in it control mechanisms to substitute for functions of a human operator. When they work they make life simpler for the user. If, however, they go wrong, it is often impossible to revert to manual operation and the equipment requires expert repair. An outstanding example of this is the self-loading film projector. Undoubtedly they are easy to operate, but if they go wrong, it can be impossible to thread them manually; and, of course, if only part of a film is required it may still be necessary to run it from the beginning to reach the part required. Automatic control can, however, be useful—for example, automatic volume control on tape recorders in the record mode, which controls increases in volume much more smoothly than a manual control, even though there is some loss of quality, but this would not be noticed in normal use.

It is also unwise to select too readily the cheapest model available. For the kind of use we are considering, more than one person will use the equipment, and robustness and ease of maintenance are more important than modest savings in the original purchase price. Finally, it is wise to restrain enthusiasm and allow innovatory equipment to run in at someone else's expense before rushing in to purchase. Many design snags are worked out of the equipment during the first year or two of its sale.

It is worth considering the relative scales of cost involved in different kinds of media, both for equipment and operation. Probably the cheapest form of audiovisual presentation is the product of simple graphics. With a supply of card, film or paper, lettering devices such as stencils or transferable typefaces and a range of coloured pens, an experienced designer can achieve great success. Elementary equipment makes this task much easier—a drawing-board speeds up the process of design, a guillotine gives a clean finish to work, T-squares, 'french curves' and so on enhance the execution of the design. By and large, however, even with a full-time designer, expenditure on graphics materials can be measured in very modest terms. But if we include under this heading reprographic services, then the cost of materials can rise enormously. Hand-operated duplicators, or even electric machines, are not expensive to buy, but they consume paper at a vast rate, especially under inexpert operation, and a strict control must be kept on paper consumption.

Photography is also a relatively cheap form of production, particularly if the unit has its own developing and printing service, but there is always a conflict over equipment. Undoubtedly, expensive cameras and lenses do provide higher quality pictures, but on the other hand the unskilled user may not be able to operate them to the best advantage. At the other end, the cassette-loaded 'snapshot' camera is ideal for convenience and simplicity of use, but may not give sufficient quality. Resolution of the problem is a matter of balancing need against cost.

An important use of photography is in the production of slides, and a simple copying stand can often be a good investment. This enables copies to be made of illustrations, drawings and even small objects quite easily and following an absolutely standard procedure. For economy, work should be accumulated so that a complete roll of film is used, and it may be sensible to prepare slides in bulk once a week or on a regular schedule. Although last minute requests can less easily be met, on the whole users seem to prefer a guaranteed day of delivery. Finally, if a printing facility with enlargers can be made available the production of large prints is a relatively cheap process. These are still not fully appreciated within education. We are so used to the small prints we obtain for domestic use that the dramatic quality of even the most ordinary print when enlarged to 10 × 8 in, or better 20 × 16 in is seldom appreciated. With modest facilities and a bit of practice the larger size prints can be produced for not many pence each, even allowing for wastage.

It is a logical progression from still photography to cine photography, but this is a development that should be approached with some caution. Modern 8mm cameras are easy to operate and relatively cheap. However, 8mm film is extremely inconvenient to handle if the results need to be edited. If there are enthusiastic and competent users (and these qualities do not necessarily go together), an investment in film equipment may be worthwhile. Certainly in some schools film-making has been found to be a very successful way of encouraging students to express themselves when more traditional methods have failed. On the other hand, portable television equipment may be even better, allowing, as it does, instant replay. This point is referred to below. As a resource 8mm film is probably of little use except in the limited form of film loops, and this is a process which has never really developed.

16mm films are in a quite different category, with an enormous number of titles available through outside libraries. The cost of 16mm production equipment is high and only larger production units would consider this process. Properly used it can produce very high quality with colour and sound, and a thoughtful comprehension of the subject which is seldom to be found in the other moving record, the videotape.

Mention of film brings in the use of sound and we should here consider this medium in its own right. Sound is clearly something of a poor relation to visual media, but the equipment, particularly using cassettes, is simple to operate, and cheap to buy. The materials are low-priced. For certain topics a good sound tape is likely to be as effective as any other form of communication, and with portable players widely owned is very accessible to students. If visuals are necessary they can be provided in the form of slides, thus producing a tape/slide programme, or in the form of an illustrated text to go with the tape. Vast amounts of valuable material are transmitted by the broadcasting companies which, subject to copyright restrictions, may be able to be recorded and made available to students. Some commercial organisations are also producing sound recordings for sale and use in libraries.

Another process which is in frequent use is the overhead projector. This particularly lends itself to the teaching of certain subjects, for example, geography, and perhaps also to certain styles of lecturing. It is not often used as a reference tool, since the transparency on its own can be better presented as an opaque print, and overlay developments perhaps as a series of prints. Nevertheless it will be a function of a resource centre to produce transparencies and the facilities need to be available.

Finally we consider television, the 'glamour' tool of the trade, and the one over which most argument has (rather unnecessarily) raged. In its early days, when only expensive professional equipment was available and the only people with experience were from broadcasting organisations, there was certainly a tendency to use television because it was there rather than because it was useful or relevant. Now the development of portable and inexpensive equipment has made it possible to use television much more informally, and we are gradually discovering uses more appropriate to study than the direct imitation of broadcast techniques. It is rather as though the only form of printed communication known to us was the newspaper or the novel, and that encyclopaedias, reference and textbooks, and even simple jottings had still to be invented. Some teachers have found television a useful way of communicating with their students. With large numbers of students lectures can be recorded and repeated *ad infinitum* or consulted later in the library. Where practical skills are to be taught television provides ideal closeup demonstrations which can be consulted privately by the student as he himself works through them. Finally, television provides a means of recording and discussing personal exchanges, and perhaps giving students some insight into their own communication difficulties. Fortunately nowadays it is possible to buy simple equipment with which one can experiment and discover some of the potential uses for television within the media organisation. Such small units can be added to until simple studio facilities are available which may be quite sufficient for most resource centres. Even so the cost of equipment is likely to be measured in at least hundreds of pounds and the cost of the videotape is also an important element.

A further development which seems likely to become increasingly widespread is the production of their own materials by students. This can serve two purposes: it gives students a different insight into a subject, for as has often been said we do not know a subject until we teach it; it also provides a source of new reference material. Although the latter may be more important in the context of this book, it is likely that educationally it is the former which is more important. Experience shows that students derive enormous pleasure, and hence probably also benefit, from working as part of a team. This is certainly necessary when they prepare materials with professional help. Indeed it seems that one of the most valuable uses of the television medium may well be to give students this experience. More than other production processes it involves people in interdependent roles, a situation which does not arise in the students' normal learning process. They enjoy the co-operation, which perhaps helps to give them the confidence to make those decisions of selection which our thesis suggests underlie all our activities.

CHAPTER VII

Storage and access

In the context of this book the word storage is used to mean the holding of material in any form in such a way of organisation that it can be found when a query arises to which it would constitute an answer.

This is, of course, the normal function of a library, and the whole profession of librarianship has been devoted to the means of fulfilling this function as efficiently as possible. However, the introduction of new media in the last twenty years seems to have encouraged librarians to think that an alien and difficult element has been introduced into their midst; although many of the fabrications of the new media have, in an earlier form, long been part of the librarian's world, some seem to have regarded the new developments as something requiring quite distinctive new techniques and even, in extreme cases, not part of their professional concern at all.

Fortunately such views are rapidly losing their currency and even in what is, perhaps justifiably, the most conservative branch of the profession, the university library, non-book materials are being accepted as resources which the librarian should take under his wing—that they are all sources of information, and need to be collected and organised if the information they contain is to be made available. They are in this fundamental respect exactly like the books which are the librarian's traditional concern.

However, the fact that they are like books does not mean they are books, and although we may apply the same principles in their organisation, the results of this application will more often than not be different. The indications are that one of the main benefits of these differences is that the librarian, who sees the applications of the same principles producing different answers, will gain a greater insight into the meaning and implication of those principles than if he had only ever applied them to books. Most of us who have moved into the world of non-book materials have gained thereby, we think, a greater understanding of what the librarianship of books is all about.

The storage of materials involves three problems. First the physical question of exactly how it is to be stored. This constitutes a serious difficulty in the case of non-book materials, since they appear in such a wide variety of formats. Secondly, there is the description of the material—cataloguing—and much effort is now being made to systematise this. Thirdly, there is the problem of classifying the material so that we shall retrieve it when it is the possible answer to our question. We will take these problems in turn.

In some ways storage seems to lie at the heart of all the difficulties we make for ourselves in organising collections of non-book materials. Most of these materials are small and packaged in such a way that they do not easily sit with books on the shelves. For the browser—a person, as Celoria[11] suggests, to be encouraged in any library—it is extremely inconvenient if the slides or sound tapes related by subject to the books he is looking through are located in a far distant corner of the library. We must however not forget that this is not a wholly new problem, since most libraries for convenience and economy shelve oversize volumes together and usually have some special collections organised quite separately. The non-book material does not therefore raise a new problem. As always, the librarian has to make a decision which will be manifest and which will inconvenience somebody. He will associate some materials with the books and he will separate others.

If the library is a new one with lots of space and perhaps limited acquisitions, the librarian will be able to be extravagant in his use of space and put all related materials together, however inconveniently they happen to associate by size. He will have some difficulty in bringing into close association the requisite equipment for using the materials. Tape recorders and slide viewers cannot be made available in an unlimited quantity. However, if these are spread evenly around the space it is likely that users will be able to refer to all the materials not too far from the point at which they are filed. As the collection expands and the space becomes more constricted, it is likely that, as with collections of books, there will be some streamlining of the organisation and the more bulky materials (those, for example, which require shelves to be set very far apart) will be stored separately. If they need special viewing equipment this will be an additional reason for doing so.

The pattern of use will also determine the pattern of organisation. Trebble[12] has suggested that all multi-media collections are in fact more usually regarded by the librarians as several single media collections. Users ask in the first place for books, films, slides, sound tapes etc on a subject. They themselves preempt the materials in which they intend to search. If this is the case, there may be little point in accumulating all materials on one subject together. Sometimes there is sufficient identity between the forms of presentation for them to be stored together. The University of Sussex Library found a significant increase in the use of microfilms when they were filed with the associated books and a reader was placed within proximity. However, the microfilm is just another form of print presentation, and clearly the seeker after books should be equally happy with a microfilm, and indeed may have to be.

It will be evident from this that although no hard and fast rules can be laid down about the storage of non-book materials, the decisions which must be made are in principle no different from those that any librarian or manager is required to make about any of the services provided. We must consider the space and equipment available, consider the pattern of use in that particular collection, and organise it accordingly.

However, having taken decisions on the organisation of the storage, it will be necessary to have regard to these when preparing the catalogue, for this, with some well designed signposts within the collection itself, will provide the 'map' of the collection.

Once again there is a question first to be decided—whether all the different materials within the library are to be contained within one catalogue, or whether there should be separate catalogues for each kind of material. Idealistically, but not necessarily ideally, the user of the catalogue should have one place to go to for information. This assumes that he is interested in material available on a given subject. But if he wants to know whether the library has a particular tape or film it will be easier for him to go to a tape or film catalogue and not have to go through dozens of references to other materials. Edge-coded or coloured cards for different materials might simplify this process, but such devices can become very complicated and difficult to remember.

One of the difficulties of separate catalogues is deciding where to draw the line. If sound records are placed separately, since for example music is obviously different from books, is it helpful to file plays and recordings of plays, or poetry and recordings of poetry separately? And if music is separate, what about scores? Such questions can only be answered, as indeed any librarian would answer them, in the context of the pattern of use of the library. If, therefore, we leave to the librarian the decision whether or not to separate the catalogues of his different materials, what view do we take on the catalogue entry itself?

There are some genuine differences between books and non-book materials which need to be borne in mind at this point. Very often the item in its non-book form is inaccessible. If it is a film it may be in a distant library; even if it is held in the local library, it is stored on a reel in a can and is invisible unless projected. The examination of single pictures conveys nothing of the film, and entirely leaves out the sound track. Sound tapes are 'unreadable'. Further, it is difficult to telescope the time-scale. Films can be speeded up a little, sound tapes or discs not at all. Therefore non-book material of this kind cannot be scanned anything like as quickly as a book. A 20-minute sound tape must be listened to for up to 20 minutes. This means that it is necessary to provide much more detailed descriptions of some items than is the case with books. On the other hand it is generally easier to look at a photograph than a book, and long descriptions of photographs are usually quite unnecessary.

Other details may be important. Films need a projector which may be 35mm or 16mm or 8mm gauge. They cannot be interchanged. Tape recordings can be made at different speeds and the player must be able to operate at the right speed. Slides can vary in size and not all projectors can take every size. It is therefore necessary to provide a good deal of physical information about non-book materials. This is no different from books. The Anglo-American Cataloguing Rules[13] provide extensively for the physical description of books. However, many libraries will be able to do without this detail. The effort to record pages, illustrations, size, etc may not be justified; but for non-book materials it becomes much more important, since without the information the material cannot be used and some of it may not be easily determined. A sound tape must be played to determine its correct speed if it is not stated on the spool.

The AACR also takes account of non-book materials. However it seems to be generally accepted that the 1967 edition does not do so effectively, and raises many more problems than it solves. One of the fundamental difficulties is the question of authorship. The rules for the cataloguing of books are based on the identification of an author, and a large number of the rules sets out to help determine the author if this is not immediately obvious. Non-book materials cannot easily be found to satisfy this rule, since either no 'author' is clearly identified and only an arbitrary choice can be made, or there are many alternative or collective persons or institutions to whom authorship can be attributed. The problem has been clarified, but certainly not resolved, in recent years as a result of discussions in the USA, Canada and Great Britain.

In America there is strong pressure to retain the concept of an author entry as the main entry of the catalogue, and if an author cannot be identified, as, for example, in the case of a film, a title entry is made as a substitute. In Britain a fundamental change was made in the approach to the catalogue entry, which was seen, not in the first place as an author entry, but rather as a description of the item in hand. This derived from the philosophy of a 'standard item description' currently being discussed in Europe as an important step in the computerisation of library records. An SID is essential if computer records are to be compatible. It must specify those aspects of the item in hand which need to be described and then allocate computer fields to them. On the whole it is not difficult to obtain agreement on these matters.

The British committee[14] considering the cataloguing of non-book materials therefore set out to determine which aspects of the different kinds of non-book materials might be needed in a catalogue description. It also suggested the sequence in which these might be set out in the entry. It is then necessary to arrange these entries in the catalogue in a way which meets the interests of the library. To do this headings are added to the description, which will provide the arrangement which the library requires.

The point should be made that although the American and British approaches are at present quite different, the results need not differ. The British view is that if in the description of the item there are identified persons or institutions which may be regarded as providing authorship, then they should be named as a heading on the standard item description. The combined statements then constitute an author entry. However this does leave open the fact that it may not be possible to identify an author, whereas the AACR regards the determination of authorship as the prime aim of a cataloguer. It is evident that the adoption of the British viewpoint would constitute a radical change in the approach to cataloguing, although not one that would materially affect the catalogue or the user in the final result. This is perhaps a case of a change of medium giving us a better insight into a subject, in this case cataloguing, with the result that in finding a solution to the cataloguing of non-book materials, we also come to a better understanding of what is required in the cataloguing of books.

If the discussion of cataloguing of non-book materials has raised technical problems, there is little doubt that the discussion of classifying them has raised great emotion. The reason is not far to seek. Most non-book materials are relatively inaccessible. They are in boxes, or cans, or cassettes. They cannot immediately be interpreted. They must be played or projected. They do not have contents lists, chapter headings or indexes. Pictures are, even in their still form, paradoxically 'invisible', since the implications of their content are likely to range far beyond the actual scenes depicted.

The librarian, who sees all such material passing unnoticed because he has not drawn attention to every possible subject reference, can easily become extremely anxious. On the other hand he has perhaps not always been equally concerned about the material 'hidden' in printed sources, and may with much less concern habitually classify a substantial book under a single Dewey number. As is so often the case, the answer may be seen to lie somewhere between the two extremes. We have of course returned to the problem of selection and retaining user confidence despite our own awareness of the information which we have not supplied.

The point is that our access to the picture or sound tape is not necessarily only through the catalogue. We have our own knowledge of the subject, as well as reference books which will enable us to come round to the headings that have been chosen.

Let us consider a photograph of the 'Pool of London' on the river Thames. It will include among many objects perhaps the Tower of London and Tower Bridge, the cruiser Belfast now moored there, wharves, now disused, general Victorian architecture, cranes, the Thames itself, and possibly small boats. We could if we wished enter it in the catalogue under all of these headings. There are also general headings like economics, for the Pool has now no commercial traffic, which has all been transferred downstream as a consequence of larger ships and containerisation. The photograph therefore could demonstrate the decline of the Pool as a commercial centre. There are librarians and teachers who would feel obliged to record the photograph under all these headings. But this is not the only approach. Let us assume we have entered it solely under 'Thames'. If we need a picture of docks we know that they are to be found in certain towns and on rivers. We would think of looking under Mersey, Liverpool, Southampton, London, Thames and so on. If we want cranes of various kinds, docks are one of the places we find them and then we follow the previous argument. If we consider practical demonstrations of economics, transport systems offer one of the manifestations of change. Transport leads us to shipping, docks, container traffic and the change in the use of docks. One of the areas of change is the Thames and we can then move to the catalogue.

The expectation that users will be able to make such a conceptual approach to the catalogue has several advantages. Firstly it is cheaper. Every entry into a catalogue costs money to prepare, to type, to file and to maintain (and to withdraw). Secondly it can be more inconvenient to use a catalogue with a great many entries than one which is streamlined. Finally there is the point already made that working out the best question to put to the collection is itself a creative process and one from which the user may benefit. Without therefore deliberately making work for the user, it should be recognised that if he can be helped by other reference tools including his own knowledge before he consults the collection, he may well be able ultimately to do so in a much more effective way.

It is a purpose of this book to urge that fundamental to the organisation of resources is the concept of exploitation. We must organise them clearly and in accordance with clear definitions. We must if possible make these clear to the user and expect him to adapt his questions to the resources available. If the question he asks is not immediately answerable within the terms of our resources, it is as much his responsibility to alter his question as it is the librarian's to adjust the approaches to his collection. There is no doubt that rephrasing the question is quite likely to result in a question which not only will be answered by the resources, but may well be a much better and more useful question to have answered. It is much to be regretted that schools in particular have been encouraged to develop very detailed cataloguing systems for their materials. Not only are they expensive to maintain, but they seem to neglect the enormous benefit children can derive from having to rephrase their questions more exactly. It gives them training in thinking and encourages them to look all round a problem, a discipline nominally recognised as important in some of the schools which install the most complicated systems.

If the point of view adumbrated above is accepted, then it is possible to use standard book classifications, but it will probably be necessary to ensure that staff are available who are skilled in the interpretation of non-book materials. They will perhaps need to be more willing to discuss problems than is sometimes the case with a librarian who is concerned only with books. But staff are needed to help readers exploit texts and not just find them.

Despite arguments against orthodox classification, there are many libraries of film materials (in some ways the most intractable material for classification) classified by UDC, and one of photographs which reverted to UDC after an experimental period with an optical coincidence system. Prints are certainly a case where minimum classification is necessary, since it is so easy to view a great many in a very short time. Further, one glance at a photograph will convey so much more than the most detailed study of a precise written description. The point made here is a simple one—limit the classification headings and provide the user with plenty of help before he consults the catalogue. It does lay the librarian open to the accusation that he has omitted to classify an item under an obvious heading, but that is a charge that he is professionally required to bear, particularly if he has provided good reference tools to back up his catalogue.

CHAPTER VIII

Conclusion

The aim of this book has been to demonstrate that the organisation of media is equivalent to the organisation of information and that it is this process which underlies all communication. Organisation as part of the process of communication sets out to state the relevant facts and to associate them one with the other within a clearly defined context. Whoever then uses the organisation or receives the communication will know how to interpret it for his own purposes. It follows therefore that there is a common objective whether we are managing a library or a resource centre or producing materials, and that this objective should extend into our own thinking and learning processes.

The considerations set out in this book have been derived from experience over many years in different kinds of libraries and in media production units, and from discussions with colleagues. However, there is no suggestion that the basic ideas are new and there are many and diverse references which give insight into this subject. Consequently it may be illuminating to mention some of the references which have helped to shape the book, and thus to provide a kind of discursive bibliography. In line with the philosophy behind the book this chapter is not intended to be a definitive text but rather to reinforce what may already be present in the reader's mind, and to suggest where he can explore related ideas with the chance that he will develop them in his own way.

One of the main themes of this book is the importance we should attach to associative thinking. We must allow ourselves and encourage those we serve to expand their ideas not only into defined channels but also in ways which seem to them to be interesting. John Holt[15] places this in a purely educational context when he says 'Children take in these word strings and store them, undigested, in their minds, so that they can spit them back out on demand. But these words do not change anything, fit with anything, relate to anything . . . How can we make school a place where real learning goes on and not just word swallowing?'

The subject of association is not a new one. Coleridge[16] in his *Biographia literaria* refers 'to the fullest and most perfect enunciation of the associative principle, viz to the writings of Aristotle; and of these in particular to the books "De anima," "De memoria," and that which is entitled in the old translations "Parva naturalia." In as much as later writers have either deviated from, or added to his doctrines, they appear to me to have introduced either error or groundless supposition.' Coleridge then idiosyncratically proceeds to consider the evolution of the idea up to his own time. I A Richards[17] (*Coleridge on imagination*) provides a commentary on the *Biographia literaria* and other related works which some may find provides easier access to Coleridge's ideas.

Bruner[18] approaches the subject from the standpoint of a contemporary psychologist. In his introduction he points out that he is enchanted by the 'fact and the symbolism of the right hand and the left—the one the doer and the other the dreamer'. He is a 'right handed psychologist' pursuing his scientific studies, but has come to recognise that these leave 'one approach unexplored. It is an approach whose medium of exchange seems to be the metaphor paid out by the left hand. It is a way that grows happy hunches and lucky guesses, that is stirred into connective activity by the poet and the necromancer looking sidewise rather than directly.' In the first part of his book he deals 'with the issue of how we know and how knowledge reflects the structuring power of the human intellect . . .' The second part entertains conjectures 'that grew, in spirit if not in original sequence, from issues raised earlier.' He goes on 'But sequence is a fiction, and in a human life what follows may have produced what went before'.

Bruner also relates the argument about the 'two cultures' to this concept of left hand/right hand ways of thinking, and argues that 'the two are not simply external ways of life, one pursued by humanists, the other by scientists. They are ways of living with one's own experience.' Professor Sir Peter Medawar[19] also refers to 'the tragedy of the two cultures' in a radio discussion on the work of Karl Popper, whose methodology he sees as completely abolishing that cultural distinction. If, as Medawar suggests, more and more scientists are accepting Popper's philosophy, it is clear that the importance of imagination in science as well as in the conventional arts is increasingly accepted. The ideas outlined in this book can then be seen as a small part of a contemporary view of the growth of knowledge.

This view can be seen in more general terms. For a century or more science has tended to be seen by scientists, and even more by the society of which they form part, as an endeavour to establish facts. Society in its anxiety for certitude invested science with an authority which its more distinguished representatives would never have expressed. As Bondi puts it in the same radio discussion, 'science is always a jumble of observation, understanding of the equipment with which the observation was carried out, interpretation and analysis. We can never clear one from another.' Now society expresses a revulsion from science which is really a revulsion from society's interpretation of science and the demands which it made on science—for example, that we should land a man on the moon. We are now rightly frightened by the unhibited logical interpretation of facts which we have encouraged science to pursue.

Auden[20] expressed this in a detailed study of Iago. He suggests that Iago 'the practical joker' is 'a parabolic figure for the autonomous pursuit of scientific knowledge through experiment which we all, whether we are scientists or not, take for granted as natural and right'. But he goes on, 'The knowledge sought by science is only one kind of knowledge'. There is the kind we mean when we say 'I know John Smith very well', but as Auden points out, 'I cannot know in this sense without being known in return. If I know John Smith well, he must also know me well. But, in the scientific sense of knowledge, I can only know that which does not and cannot know me.' He concludes: 'To apply a categorical imperative to knowing, so that, instead of asking, "What can I know?" we ask, "What, at this moment, am I meant to know?"—to entertain the possibility that the only knowledge which can be true for us is the knowledge we can live up to—that seems to all of us crazy and almost immoral. But, in that case, who are we to say to Iago—"No, you mustn't".'

The danger is that if society accepts the view of Auden and turns towards an imaginative and intuitive view of society it will lose not only what is bad in science but what is good as well. Ornstein[21] describes our different ways of thinking as the rational and intuitive approaches. He particularly emphasises the importance to our survival of a linear, rational approach which he regards as 'essential for an organised culture.' There are certain things we must know if we are to be able to continue as members of our society. For him science constitutes 'a highly specialised development of consciousness, at once its most conservative, yet its most reliable'. He goes on, 'most cultures are fundamentally based on this active, linear mode—the way of language, science and history. Ours is so thoroughly based on it that many have almost forgotten that other constructions of individual consciousness, other cultural styles are even possible.'

This point is, incidentally, beautifully illustrated by a quotation used by Foucalt[22] to describe how his book, *The order of things*, 'first arose out of a passage in Borges, out of the laughter that shattered, as I read the passage, all the familiar landmarks of my thought—*our* thought, the thought that bears the stamp of our age and our geography—breaking up all the ordered surfaces and all the planes with which we are accustomed to tame the wild profusion of existing things, and continuing long afterwards to disturb and threaten with collapse our age-old distinction between the Same and the Other. This passage quotes a "certain Chinese encyclopaedia" in which it is written that "animals are divided into: (a) belonging to the Emperor, (b) embalmed, (c) tame, (d) sucking pigs, (e) sirens, (f) fabulous, (g) stray dogs, (h) included in the present classification, (i) frenzied, (j) innumerable, (k) drawn with a very fine camelhair brush, (l) *et cetera*, (m) having just broken the water pitcher, (n) that from a long way off look like flies". In the wonderment of this taxonomy, the thing we apprehend in one great leap, the thing that, by means of the fable, is demonstrated as the exotic charm of another system of thought, is the limitation of our own, the stark impossibility of thinking *that*.'

Ornstein[23] really takes the point that Foucault is making, and asks that we should accept the importance of rational thinking, but that we should also seek to strengthen our intuitive processes which will enable us to see alternative interpretations of the facts which surround us. He describes experiments which seem to show that the two halves of the brain specialise in different kinds of thinking. 'The left hemisphere (connected to the right side of the body) is predominantly involved with analytical, logical thinking especially in verbal and mathematical functions. Its mode of operation is primarily linear.' The right hemisphere 'is primarily responsible for our orientation in space for artistic endeavour, crafts, body image, recognition of faces. It processes information more diffusely than does the left hemisphere and its responsibilities demand a ready integration of many inputs at once.' He refers to the complementarity of the two major modes of consciousness and we shall return to this phrase later.

The experimental evidence of Ornstein is an invaluable adjunct to the feeling that many people have had that the human brain does have these dual qualities, for example, the essay by Bruner referred to earlier. There is also an essay by Aldous Huxley[24] which emphasises the limitations of language (*ie*, linear thinking) and the importance of a non-verbal curriculum. He quotes two poems by Wordsworth. *Expostulation and reply* and *The tables turned* in which the two modes of thinking are described. He urges with Wordsworth 'that we can feed this mind of ours in a wise passiveness'.

Two other essays, both by Kubie,[25],[26] deserve mention in this context, 'The forgotten man of education' and 'Research in protecting preconscious functions in education.' The 'forgotten man' is oneself, and Kubie urges the importance of self-knowledge in education for, as his second essay says, the conscious component is but a sample of the total thinking. Thinking is a preconscious process and our conscious sampling process is but a weighted fragment of the whole in which we determine the weighting. Knowledge of ourselves is vital if we are to understand our thinking. As Proust[27] puts it, 'It is our passions which draw the outline of our books; the ensuing intervals of repose which write them'. (Ce sont nos passions qui esquissent nos livres; le repos d'intervalle qui les écrit.)

I A Richards[28] has always concerned himself with meaning, and his collection of essays *Speculative instruments* deals particularly with aspects of interpretation, which is of course a form of association. In considering the future of the humanities he remarks, in line with Ornstein, that our 'minds have become more exposed than ever before'. Whilst he acknowledges the contribution of modern scholarship in providing us with more and more information, he suggests that 'for the time being its present dangers rather than its remote promises should concern us most'. Our greatest need as he sees it 'is teachers able to help humanity remain humane'. He suggests in a further essay 'Language and value'[29] that 'to a much greater extent than we profess we communicate through offerings of choices, not through presentations of fact'. It is surely clear that any library, resource centre or media production is offering just such a choice of interpretations by the way in which it organises the information it has at its disposal.

(Richards[30] makes a similar point in *Science and poetry* when he describes how experience takes up only some impressions, and he draws attention to the fact that 'many other impressions all day long remain entirely unnoticed because no interest responds to them'.)

Writings about music or, perhaps even more so, our thoughts about music often give an insight into this view of communication. Music is, after all, one of the most pervasive of languages and its very pervasiveness gives us insights into the processes of communication. Interpretation is naturally regarded as an essential part of music, and we recognise that each interpreter is indeed communicating to us a different understanding of the music. Each interpreter is associating the same notes in a different way, and it is the opportunity it provides for these differences of association which make music such a universal language. We know and accept that music is capable of different interpretations and we must develop the same flexibility in our reaction to all communication.

Schnabel is one musician who had a gift for evocative turns of phrase, some of which were repeated by Clifford Curzon,[31] a student of Schnabel, in a recent interview. He expected his students to build their own interpretations from his lessons and, as Curzon put it, 'it was his insight into what lies behind and between the written notes of the greatest music that made his teaching so invaluable'. Curzon tells the story of Schnabel, asked to re-record the opening of the Brahms B Flat concerto because of some confused octave passage, remarking 'I may play better but it won't be as good'. Curzon remarks that this paradox makes perfectly good sense to a musician. It is the purpose of this book to help it make sense to managers of resources.

The library may be better organised but will it be as good a library? We may know how we could make the catalogue or the classification more extensive (*ie*, approach perfection), but would it necessarily be more helpful to the user or would he be confused by the additional information? The film could certainly contain more information, but would it necessarily be then more comprehensible? Our aim must surely be not perfection but simplicity and clarity, for we cannot hope to achieve and should not want to achieve a complete identity with the ideas of the user.

John Ruskin's[32] criticism of the Renaissance is in some ways based on this attitude. He says 'But when this perfection (of Ghirlandaio, Bellini and others) had once been exhibited in anything, it was required in everything; the world could no longer be satisfied with less exquisite execution, or less disciplined knowledge. The first thing that it demanded in all work was, that it should be done in a consummate and learned way; and men altogether forgot that it was possible to consummate what was contemptible, and to know what was useless.' He goes on to point out that the attack of the Renaissance upon Gothic schools had 'more fatal and immediate (results) in architecture . . . because there the demand for perfection was less reasonable, and less consistent with the capabilities of the workman!'. In his essay on the 'Nature of Gothic'[33] he considers the role of the workman: 'Men were not intended to work with the accuracy of tools, to be precise and perfect in all their actions. If you will have that degree of precision out of them, and make their fingers measure degrees like cog-wheels, and their arms strike curves like compasses, you must unhumanise them.'

Richards[34] in his *Speculative instruments* postulates a related idea: 'The properties of the instruments or apparatus employed enter into, contribute to, belong with and confine the scope of the investigation'. Ruskin is making the point that the workman must be taken into account when we design a piece of architecture, and Lessing[35] is raising the same question when he considers the differences in the way the story of Laokoon is portrayed in the sculpture and in Virgil's poem. Richards, however, draws his comparison from physics. He quotes from J R Oppenheimer's formulation of Bohr's Principle of Complementarity: 'The basic finding was that in the atomic world it is not possible to describe the atomic system under investigation in abstraction from the apparatus used for the investigation by a single, unique objective model. Rather, a variety of models, each corresponding to a possible experimental arrangement and all required for a complete description of possible physical experience, stand in a complementary relation to one another, in that the actual realisation of any one model excludes the realisation of others, yet each is a necessary part of the complete description of experience in the atomic world. It is . . . not yet fully clear how characteristically or how frequently we shall meet instances . . . in other fields, above all in the study of biological, psychological and cultural problems.' (Richards[36] incidentally expanded on the theme of complementarity in a lecture given in 1972.)

Bohr[37] enunciated his Principle of Complementarity when he was asked in 1927 to give a report on the epistemological problems confronting quantum physics. It was designed in part to take account of Heisenberg's Principle of Uncertainty. As Bronowski[38] puts it, 'early that year (1927) Heisenberg gave a new characterisation of the electron'. It was a particle but one which yielded limited information. 'You can specify where it is at this instant, but then you cannot impose on it a specific speed and direction at the setting-off.'

Further, 'Heisenberg gave (this characterisation) depth by making it precise (in mathematical terms)'. However, Bronowski feels 'the Principle of Uncertainty is a bad name. In science or outside it, we are not uncertain: our knowledge is merely confined within a certain tolerance. We should call it the Principle of Tolerance. . . . First, in the engineering sense . . . because (science) has understood that the exchange of information between man and nature and man and man, can only take place with a certain tolerance. But second . . . all knowledge, all information between human beings, can only be exchanged within a play of tolerance.'

Bohr[39] himself had foreseen the implications of his principle for other areas of knowledge. In 1932 he said, 'the necessity of considering the interaction between the measuring instruments and the object under investigation in atomic mechanics exhibits a close analogy to the peculiar difficulties in psychological analysis arising from the fact that the mental content is invariably altered when attention is concentrated on any special feature of it'.

It is interesting that 40 years later Liam Hudson[40] says that psychologists 'could follow the example of Heisenberg and physicists: retain our concern for truth, but accept that even the most disinterested attempts to measure the natural world are bound to alter it—that, in our case, the assessments we attempt of other people may influence them in profound and harmful ways'. He is concerned with the relationship between measurable facts and human behaviour and concludes, 'I feel the need for a view of knowledge, and a means of expressing that view, which will imply that the contents of the mind matter'. Surely the failure of the educational psychologists to meet this need is one of the principal reasons for the low status that Bruner[41] suggests they now enjoy.

Hudson[42] recognises the ambiguity of the teacher's role in education. 'It would seem that the teacher who leaves his students' minds open, in a state of promiscuous athleticism, is scarcely a teacher at all. His proper function, in other words must be an ambiguous one: he must transmit an intellectual tradition with gusto, and instil loyalty to it, but leave open the possibility of gradual or even revolutionary change. And what matters in practice is not so much the teacher's motive, nor even his style, as the elbow room he allows.'

This surely is the central issue we have been discussing throughout this book. How can we achieve the right balance between information and imagination? The ambiguity exists not just in the teacher's role but in education itself, because, in establishing education, society itself produced a dilemma. On the one hand it needs to train people to take their place in society to follow the existing pattern, whilst on the other it recognises and accepts what will happen in any case, that people will interpret that training in their own way and unavoidably the process of education will have laid the foundations for change. What that change will be we cannot know and we must learn to live with that uncertainty. Our problem is to do this whilst at the same time training for continuity.

Managers of resources face this problem in concrete material terms. They are required to organise those materials and can only do so in terms of the ideas and associations that have produced them. Only the future can tell us to what uses they will then be applied. For managers the uncertainties should be tangible, for it is the use to which the objects are put that counts, and the managers task is to ensure that they can be used as flexibly and unrestrictedly as possible.

W D Wall[43] has written perhaps the best closing sentences which could be found for this book: 'The heart and soul of a resources collection is not material at all: it lies in the structures of thought it exhibits, in the creative associations it provokes and in the opportunities it provides for training the young learner in how to learn and to think'.

References

1 Comenius, J A: *Orbis sensualim pictus*. Facsimile ed. Sydney University Press 1967.

2 Richards, I A: *The philosophy of rhetoric*. OUP, New York 1971, p10.

3 Heath, S A: 'Conversation with Roland Barthes' *in Signs of the times*. Granta Publications, Cambridge 197?, p43.

4 Saussure, F de: *Course in general linguistics*. Fontana, London 1974, p111 *et seq*.

5 Richards, I A: *op cit* p27.

6 Saussure, F de: *op cit* p123.

7 Ornstein, R E: 'In two minds'. *Psychology today* (UK) vol 1 no 2 May 1975, pp40–43.

8 Ludlam, F H: 'The meteorology of Shelley's ode'. *Times literary supplement* no 3679 1 Sept 1972, pp1015–1016.

9 Sidney, P: *A defence of poetry*. OUP, London 1966, p32.

10 Chibnall, B *et al: The use of film in university teaching*. Media Service Unit, University of Sussex 1973.

11 Celeria, F: 'The archaeology of serendip'. *Library Association record* vol 70 no 10 October 1968, pp251–253.

12 Trebble, T: *The impact of new media on libraries*. Second interim report on OSTI project SI/57/09.

13 *Anglo-American cataloguing rules*. Library Association, London 1967.

14 Non-book materials cataloguing rules. National Council for

Educational Technology with the Library Association, London 1973.

15 Holt, J: *How children fail*. Pitman, New York, 1964, p107.

16 Coleridge, S T: *Biographia literaria*. OUP, London 1907, p71.

17 Richards, I A: *Coleridge on imagination*. Routledge & Kegan Paul, London 1968.

18 Bruner, J S: *On knowing—essays for the left hand*. Belknap Press, Cambridge, Mass 1962, p2 *et seq.*

19 'The achievement of Sir Karl Popper'. *The listener* vol 88 no 2265 24 Aug 1972, pp225–229.

20 Auden, W H: 'The joker in the pack' in *The dyer's hand and other essays*. Faber and Faber, London 1975, pp270 *et seq.*

21 Ornstein, R: *The psychology of consciousness*. Cape, London 1975, pp40–41.

22 Foucault, M: *The order of things*. Tavistock, London 1970, pxv.

23 Ornstein, R: *op cit*, pp51–52.

24 Huxley, A: 'Education on the non-verbal level' in *Contemporary educational psychology*, R M Jones (ed). Harper Torchbooks, New York 1967, p51 *et seq.*

25 Kubie, L S: 'The forgotten man of education' in *Contemporary educational psychology*, R M Jones (ed). Harper Torchbooks, New York 1967, pp61–71.

26 Kubie, L S: 'Research in protecting preconscious functions in education' in *Contemporary educational psychology*, R M Jones (ed). Harper Torchbooks, New York 1967, pp72–88.

27 Proust, M: *Time regained*, part 2. Chatto and Windus, London 1970, p279.

28 Richards, I A: *Speculative instruments*. Routledge & Kegan Paul, London 1955, p58 *et seq.*

29 Richards, I A: *Science and poetry*. Routledge & Kegan Paul, London 1970, p29.

29 Richards, I A: *Speculative instruments*. Routledge & Kegan Paul, London 1955, p139.

30 Richards, I A: *Science and poetry*. Routledge & Kegan Paul, London 1970, p29.

31 'Artur Schnabel pianist and teacher—Clifford Curzon talks to Alan Blyth.' *The listener* vol 91 no 2352 25 April 1974, pp544–546.

32 Ruskin, J: *The stones of Venice*, vol 3. George Allen & Unwin, London 1925, p11.

33 Ruskin, J: *op cit* vol 2. p159.

34 Richards, I A: *Speculative instruments*. Routledge & Kegan Paul, London 1955, p114 *et seq*.

35 Lessing, G E: *Laokoon*. G Bell & Sons, London 1904.

36 Richards, I A: *Complementarities*. Birkbeck College, London 1972.

37 Bohr, N: *Essays 1958–1962 on atomic physics and human knowledge*. Interscience Publishers, New York 1963, p91.

38 Bronowski, J: *The ascent of man*. BBC, London, 1973, p364–365.

39 Bohr, N: *Atomic physics and human knowledge*. Wiley, New York 1958, p11.

40 Hudson, L: *The cult of the fact*. Jonathan Cape, London 1972, pp134 & 177.

41 Bruner, J: 'Education as social invention' *in Contemporary educational psychology*, R M Jones (ed). Harper Torchbooks, New York 1967, p42.

42 Hudson, L: *The cult of the fact*. Jonathan Cape, London 1972, pp98–99.

43 Wall, W D: 'Libraries as resources in schools'. *The school librarian* vol 22 no 2 June 1974, pp117–125.

Index

Association, process of
   Brain function, 18
   Communication, 11
   Linguistics, 15, 18
   Meaning, 14
   Resource collections, 75
   Structures, 14
Associative thinking, 66, 70
Audiovisual unit, definition, 23

Brain function, 18

Career structure, 42, 46
Cataloguers, 34, 44
Cataloguing media, 58 et seq, 71
Centralisation of resources, 35
Choice, importance of, 79 et seq
Cinephotography, 51
Classification of media, 61 et seq, 71
Classifiers, 34, 45
Clerical staff, 35, 39, 47
Communication
   Association, 15
   Context, 15
   Spaces, 11, 26
Complementarity, 73
Consultancy, 22, 31 et seq, 37, 39

Differences, creative effect, 27

Education
   Instruction, 12
   Panaceas, 29
Equipment for production, 49 et seq
Exploitation of resources, 63

Film making, 51

Graphic design, 50
Graphic designers, 35, 45
   Role in education, 37

Heisenberg Uncertainty Principle, 73

Iago (Othello), 67
Imagination
   in education, 74 et seq
   in science, 67
Information
   Association, 10
   Imagination, 74
   Relentless pursuit of, 67
   Structure, 11
Instruction
   Education, 12
Interpretation, 11, 14 et seq, 71

Johnson, Samuel, 17

Learner
   Personal structure, 15
   Processes, 28 et seq
Left-hand right-hand thinking, 18, 66, 69
Libraries
   Attitudes of teachers, 10
   Consultancy role, 22
   Definition, 22
   Use by teachers, 30
Librarians
   Attitude to using resources, 43
   Comparison with graphic designers, 37
   Comparison with producers, 39 et seq
Linear thinking, 18
Linguistics, 15, 18

Media
   Cataloguing, 58 et seq
   Classification, 61 et seq
   Packaging, 56
   Structure, 15
Multimedia collections, 57

Needs of users
   Balanced with cost, 25

Matching to resources, 31

Panaceas in education, 29
Photography, 50
Producers
    Attitude to resources, 43
    Comparison with librarians, 40
    Qualifications, 39
Psychology in education, 74

Questions and answers
    Creative interaction, 27
    Danger of perfection, 28, 71, 72
    Example of fairy story, 29

Renaissance, 72
Resource centre, definition, 22
Resources
    Exploitation, 63
    Librarian attitudes, 43
    Matching to needs, 31, 35
    Producer attitudes, 43
    Teacher attitudes, 10
Routine procedures, 24

Selection, 13, 70
Services
    Organisation, 38
    Procedures, 24
Shelley, Percy Bysshe, 19

Sound recording, 52
Space in production units, 48
Spaces in communication, 11, 26, 69, 71
Students experience of production, 53
Structure
    Association, 11
    Context, 21
    Expression, 19
    Information, 12
    Learner, 15
    Medium, 15
    Role of media, 23
    Routine procedures, 24
    Teacher, 15
    Use in questions and answers, 33

Teachers
    Attitudes to resources, 10
    Personal structure, 15
    Role, 28 *et seq*
    Use of libraries, 30
Technical staff
    Creative role, 44 *et seq*
    Definition, 34, 39
Television, 52
Thinking
    Associative, 66, 70
    Linear, 18

Uncertainty Principle, 73